CHARMED

A Fresh Twist on
CHARM QUILTS

JODI CROWELL

Martingale®
& COMPANY

DEDICATION

To Barry, for your encouragement, support, patience, and love. Thank you.

ACKNOWLEDGMENTS

Thank you to Candace Eisner Strick, whose book *The Quilter's Quick Reference Guide* (Martingale & Company, 2004) contains a wealth of information for both beginning and accomplished quilters.

Thank you also to the staff of Martingale & Company whose quick and helpful replies to my questions made writing this book an enjoyable, and much less daunting, experience.

Charmed: A Fresh Twist on Charm Quilts
© 2007 by Jodi Crowell

That Patchwork Place® is an imprint of Martingale & Company®.

Martingale & Company
20205 144th Ave. NE
Woodinville, WA 98072-8478 USA
www.martingale-pub.com

Credits

President & CEO: Tom Wierzbicki
Publisher: Jane Hamada
Editorial Director: Mary V. Green
Managing Editor: Tina Cook
Developmental Editor: Karen Costello Soltys
Technical Editor: Nancy Mahoney
Copy Editor: Candie Frankel
Design Director: Stan Green
Assistant Design Director: Regina Girard
Illustrator: Robin Strobel
Cover & Text Designer: Stan Green
Photographer: Brent Kane

Printed in China
12 11 10 09 08 07   8 7 6 5 4 3 2 1

Library of Congress Cataloging-in-Publication Data
Library of Congress Control Number: 2007028089

ISBN: 978-1-56477-774-4

MISSION STATEMENT

Dedicated to providing quality products and service to inspire creativity.

CONTENTS

Introduction ... 3

Building a Charm-Square
    Collection ... 4

Quiltmaking Basics ... 6

Starflower ... 10

Simply Charming ... 14

Interlocking Squares ... 17

Hearts and Flowers ... 20

Color in Layers ... 25

Pretty in Pink ... 29

INTRODUCTION

The memories of my childhood are cozily wrapped in quilts and vintage cotton prints. I remember playing amongst bolts of fabric while my grandmother shopped, sorting through her wonderful collection of scraps on rainy afternoons, and, ultimately, sleeping under one of her wonderful hand-stitched creations. These memories left an indelible impression, fostering in me a lifelong love and appreciation of quilts and fabric. They inspired me to tap into my own creative nature and become a quilter myself. Some people suggest my quilting has grown into an addiction, and I would happily agree. I take comfort in the thought that there are others like me—quilters who select vacation spots based on their proximity to quilt shops, who prefer the scent of freshly washed and ironed cotton to the finest of perfumes.

I find collecting fabric and building a stash to be as enjoyable as cutting and stitching it into a quilt. But no matter how large my collection becomes, there is always that missing elusive fabric that would be perfect for my latest project. With the overwhelming selection of fabrics available today, it's impossible to purchase all of the fabric we want (or *think* we need) to transform our projects from ordinary to spectacular.

Charm squares are a practical and inexpensive way to increase your fabric choices. They are truly a quilter's delight. In this book, charm squares are used to add variety. They help impart the wonderfully "scrappy" appeal of traditional Charm quilts, which were created using a single pattern piece and following the rule that no fabric be repeated.

An existing collection of charm squares was the inspiration for some of the quilts in this book, while others, like "Pretty in Pink" on page 29, required me to expand my collection (as if a quilter needs an excuse to buy more fabric!). These quilts capture the essence of traditional Charm quilts while redefining them with the use of duplicate fabrics, more than one pattern piece, and appliquéd accents.

Whether you already have a stack of charm squares waiting to be stitched into one of these patterns, or are inspired to start a new collection, I think you'll enjoy all aspects of using charm squares to enhance your quilted creations. The wonderful little squares capture a piece of quilter's paradise, where fabric stashes are limitless and our quilts sparkle with color. Happy quilting!

—Jodi Crowell

BUILDING A CHARM-SQUARE COLLECTION

Traditionally, Charm quilts were made using just one pattern piece (such as a hexagon) and cutting each patch from a different fabric. Lacking the resources available to modern quilters to attain a vast and varied fabric collection, the long-ago quilter called upon family and friends to share their fabric bounty. Possessing a timeless appeal, Charm quilts have been part of the quilting world for over a century.

Collecting charm squares is a fun and easy way to build and enhance your fabric stash. Whether you use charm squares in a conventional way or go in a more contemporary direction, as do the projects in this book, the squares are sure to infuse your quilting with color and diversity. There is no standard size for charm squares. If you don't already possess a collection, you'll most likely want to build your collection based on the size required for a specific project, whether it's a tiny 2" square or a more substantial 6" square.

The project instructions in this book list the amount and minimum size of charm squares required along with any additional yardage needed to complete the project. To make the quilts in this book, you'll need charm squares in different sizes, from 2⅞" to 4".

Regardless of size, charm squares add sparkle to your quilts!

Acquiring Charm Squares

There are several routes to acquiring charm squares.

Build your own stash. Trim those odd-sized fabric scraps into the squares or shapes required for your project. An excellent way to enjoy treasured fat quarters or larger pieces of yardage is to cut a few squares from each and use them in several projects.

Shop at quilt and fabric stores. Many shops carry bundles of charm squares in varying sizes, colors, and themes. If they aren't available at your local shop, suggest that they start carrying them. Online quilt shops are another excellent source, and don't forget to browse the classifieds in your favorite quilt magazine.

Attend charm-square swaps. Swaps are so much fun and a great way to build your collection. If you can't find a swap within your circle of quilting friends and family members, start one.

Organizing a Charm Swap

Swap guidelines are absolutely essential for a successful swap. A hostess is responsible for ensuring that the swap runs smoothly. First and foremost is deciding when and how to distribute the charm squares to each member. Specify a "sign up before" date so that you know exactly who is participating in a given month, and a "deliver by" date so that everyone receives their squares at the same time. Try to adhere to the same schedule every month.

In some swaps, the hostess collects one or more sets of identical squares from each participant. The number of squares in each set is determined by how many people participate. She then divides the squares equally among the members, adding, of course, her own squares and keeping one finished set for herself. For example, if 10 people, including the hostess, have decided to exchange two sets of squares, each person would choose two fabrics, cut 10 squares from each fabric, and send these 20 squares (two sets of 10) to the hostess. This swap plan would result in all participants

Charm squares were born of necessity, when one of our quilting foremothers embarked upon a journey to create a quilt using hundreds—possibly thousands—of different fabrics.

receiving 20 different squares, including 2 squares in their own original fabrics. Participants should include postage for each set the hostess would have to mail out to members.

Another way to conduct a swap is for the hostess to distribute a list of each participant's name and address to each member. Members are then responsible for sending out their own sets. Perhaps 10 members have decided to trade 10 squares of assorted prints. Each person would prepare and send a set of 10 different squares to each participant on the list (except, of course, herself) and would in turn receive 9 sets, each with 10 assorted squares. This method works well for a swap involving a smaller number of participants.

Some other things to consider are:

Size

Choose the size of squares you wish to swap and specify a preference for rotary-cut fabric. This is especially important if you plan to use the squares as is and have no room for error. However, you can always request a size ½" larger than what you actually need to allow for individual differences in cutting.

Color

If you decide to make your swap a monthly event, choose a different color and/or theme each time. Maybe you require blue charm squares for your project so you choose blue as the color for the first swap. Permit a different member to choose the color and/or theme for each month. You can limit the swap to solids, tone-on-tone prints, or other prints, or you might want some of each in a particular color. You can ask for fabrics that are light, medium, or dark in value, or you can ask for some of each.

Quality

All fabric should be 100% cotton only and should be machine washed in warm water and detergent (no fabric softener!), dried, and pressed before cutting. Stress the importance of prewashing fabric before cutting it into squares to everyone in your charm swap. Exchange only what you would like to receive in return.

Quantity

The quantity to swap can be decided by the group—just keep the amount realistic for everyone. If you have a large swap group, it may not be feasible to exchange 50 squares at a time. On the other hand, if your group is small, exchanging only a few squares each time can be frustrating if you are trying to acquire a large collection of a specific color. Also, be prepared to receive duplicates; not everyone has a huge selection of a particular color in their stash or access to a large variety of fabrics at their local quilt shop.

UGLY DUCKLINGS

Don't overlook the "ugly ducklings" of the fabric world. Often it's the loud, eye-popping colors and prints that give quilts, particularly scrappy Charm quilts, their visual appeal. If you participate in a charm swap, you'll probably receive lots of ugly ducklings! Used in small amounts, these less attractive prints and colors are fine.

If you don't know enough fellow quilters to make a swap worthwhile, consider an online swap. Do a search for charm swaps and see what you find. Many online quilt groups are involved in charm swaps and are usually very welcoming and open to new members. If you're unfamiliar with these groups, learn about online etiquette and be aware of any rules listed by an individual group before joining and posting any information. Always exercise caution and common sense when the exchange of personal information is involved. In the event you can't find an online group that suits you, create your own group and use the guidelines for charm-square swapping described above. Above all else, have fun!

QUILTMAKING BASICS

This section provides a quick overview of the basic skills needed to make the quilts in this book. For more guidance on any of the following techniques, refer to *The Quilter's Quick Reference Guide* by Candace Eisner Strick (Martingale & Company, 2004).

Templates

You'll need to make templates for some of the pieces that cannot be rotary cut. Template patterns are given with the projects that require them. All of the patterns are full-sized, unless indicated otherwise.

Depending on the technique used to stitch the pieces, the template pattern may or may not include seam allowances. The seam allowance will be shown if it is part of the template. Seam allowances are not included on templates for appliqué pieces.

Template plastic is essential for accurate tracing. To make a template, place a piece of template plastic over the required pattern. Use a fine-tip permanent marker to trace the lines of the shape exactly onto the plastic. If the pattern has a fabric grain line, mark the line on the template. Use utility scissors to cut out the template *exactly* on the drawn lines. Mark the right side of the template. You need to make only one plastic template for each different pattern piece.

Appliqué

Appliqué can transform a perfectly ordinary quilt into something spectacular. It can easily be accomplished using the freezer-paper method described below, which is my favorite. Freezer paper is sold in most supermarkets. It is a white, heavy paper, dull on one side and shiny on the reverse. Be sure to purchase paper that is plastic coated.

In freezer-paper appliqué, you cut individual templates from freezer paper, iron them to the fabric, and then use the edge of the template as a guide to turn under a seam allowance. Because you'll be pressing the freezer-paper template to the wrong side of your fabric, the image must be reversed to start. For symmetrical shapes, this isn't a concern, but if the shape is asymmetrical, be sure to place the plastic template right side down onto the dull side of the freezer paper before tracing.

1. Make a plastic template for each shape. Flip each plastic template *right side* down onto the dull side of the freezer paper and trace around it. Or, if you prefer, you can trace the pattern directly onto the dull side of the freezer paper by placing the pattern right side down on a light box or light-filled window. Place the freezer paper shiny side down on top of the pattern and trace around the pattern with a pencil. This method is handy when you only need to make a few of each shape.

2. Cut out each freezer-paper template exactly on the drawn line. Do not add a seam allowance.

3. Place the shiny side of the freezer-paper template on the wrong side of the chosen fabric. Press with a hot, dry iron.

4. Cut out the fabric shape, leaving a scant ¼" seam allowance around the paper template as you cut.

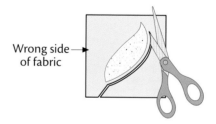

Wrong side of fabric

5. Using the edge of the paper template as a guide, fold the excess fabric allowance over onto the freezer paper and hand baste it in place. Do not remove the paper template. Or, if you prefer, you can do as I do and iron the seam allowance toward the dull side of the paper template, using small amounts of spray starch to hold the seam allowance in place. I like to remove the paper template at this time.

6. Pin or baste the appliqué pieces to the background fabric. The order in which the pieces should be appliquéd is indicated on the patterns. Stitch the pieces in place using a traditional appliqué stitch and matching thread color. Pull the needle through the background, catching only a few threads on the edge of the appliqué shape. Keep the stitches very small and work from right to left (or left to right if you're left-handed).

7. Remove the pins or basting stitches. Carefully cut a slit in the background fabric behind the appliqué shape and remove the paper template. Take care not to cut into the appliquéd shape. (If you removed the paper template in step 5, you don't need to cut a slit in the background fabric.)

Bias Stems and Vines

A bias bar is a long, thin metal or plastic strip. This time-saving tool helps you make stems of a uniform width.

Bias bars come in a variety of widths; choose the bias bar width that corresponds to the finished width of your stem. Cut *bias* strips of fabric twice this width plus ½" for seam allowances. For example, if your finished stem is ⅜" wide, then cut a bias strip 1¼" wide. To cut bias strips, use your longest rotary ruler and line up the 45° angle line with the selvage.

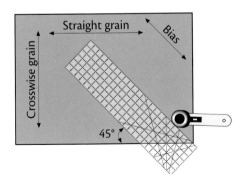

Cut one or more bias strips in the required width to achieve the length needed for the quilt you are making. You may need to piece several strips together to obtain the desired length. To do this, place the strips right

sides together, offsetting them by ¼". Stitch together, leaving a ¼" seam allowance. Press the seams open to minimize bulk.

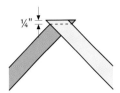

1. Fold the fabric strip in half lengthwise, *wrong* sides together, and sew a scant ¼" from the raw edges. For very narrow stems, you may need to trim the seam allowance.

2. Slide the bias bar inside the fabric tube. Twist the fabric until the seam is centered on one side of the bar. Press the tube flat with the seam allowance to one side. Be careful—metal bars can get very hot during pressing. Continue sliding the bias bar inside the tube, pressing as you go, until you've pressed the entire tube. Remove the bias bar and press the tube again.

3. Cut the fabric tube to your required stem or vine length. Position the cut sections on your background fabric, pin in place, and stitch with matching thread.

Quarter-Circle Units

Several of the quilts in this book are assembled using quarter-circle units. These units are similar to the traditional Drunkard's Path block but are made using a freezer-paper appliqué technique to eliminate sewing a curved seam.

To make a quarter-circle unit, you'll need two squares. One square will be used for the quarter-circle shape and the other square will be used for the appliqué background.

1. Trace and cut the number of quarter-circle freezer-paper templates indicated for the quilt you are making. The quarter-circle pattern includes a ¼" seam allowance along the straight edges; do not add a seam allowance along the curved edge.

2. Align the straight edges of a freezer-paper template from step 1 with two cut edges of a quarter-circle fabric square as shown. Press using a hot, dry iron.

3. Cut out the shape, leaving a scant ¼" seam allowance along the curved edge.

4. Hand baste or press the seam allowance along the curved edge toward the template.

5. Align the straight edges of the quarter-circle shape with the edges of the background fabric square. Pin in place and stitch the curved edge with matching thread.

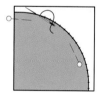

6. Remove the basting stitches and paper template, if present. Trim away the background fabric from behind the quarter-circle shape, leaving a ¼" seam allowance beyond the appliqué stitches.

Binding Your Quilt

Some of the quilts in this book use straight-grain binding, while others require bias binding for ease of stitching around curved edges. The difference in making the two types of binding is merely in how you cut the strips. After that, they are sewn together and attached to the quilt in the same manner.

I like to use single-fold binding to finish the quilt edges. For the quilts in this book, I used 2"-wide strips, for a ½"-wide finished binding.

1. To make one long, continuous strip, join the strips with a diagonal seam, as shown in "Bias Stems and Vines" on page 7. If necessary, trim the excess fabric, leaving a ¼"-wide seam. Press the seams open.

2. Fold the long binding strip in half lengthwise, wrong sides together, and press. Then, fold in each cut edge toward the first fold, wrong sides together, and press again.

3. Unfold the binding strip. Position the binding strip on the quilt, right sides together, aligning one cut edge of the binding with the raw edge of the quilt. Starting in the center of one side, and beginning about 1" from the strip's end, sew through all three layers with a ½" seam allowance, using the fold as a guide. Stop ½" from the first corner and backstitch.

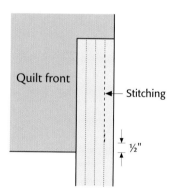

4. Remove the quilt from the machine. Turn the quilt and fold the binding straight up. Fold the binding back down, aligning it with the edge of the next side. Begin with a backstitch at the fold of the binding and continue sewing down the next side. Treat the next corner in the same way. Continue in this way around all four corners.

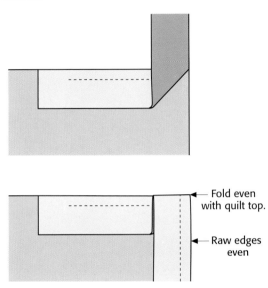

Fold even with quilt top.

Raw edges even

5. Stop sewing approximately 4" from the starting point. Fold back the beginning tail ½" and overlap the ending tail with the ½" folded edge. Trim away any excess binding. Then continue stitching to hold all three layers in place.

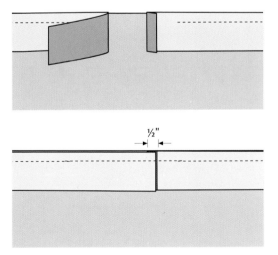

½"

6. Fold the binding over the raw edges to the back of the quilt. Sew the pressed edge of the binding to the back of the quilt by hand, using a slip stitch and matching thread. Miter each of the corners as shown.

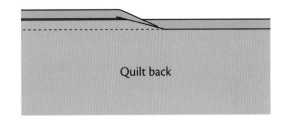

Quilt back

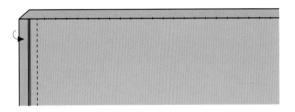

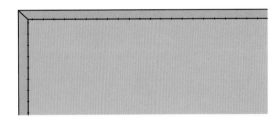

ROUNDED EDGES

To bind rounded edges, you'll need to use bias binding. Cut bias strips as shown in "Bias Stems and Vines" on page 7. Apply the binding as described in "Binding Your Quilt" on page 8. Of course, you won't have corners to miter, but the other steps for attaching and finishing the binding are the same.

Be sure to gently ease the binding around the curves, taking care not to stretch it as you sew. For excellent guidance regarding all aspects of applying binding to rounded edges, see *Happy Endings* by Mimi Dietrich (Martingale & Company, 2003).

STARFLOWER

Gather your prettiest charm squares! As easy to piece as it is feminine, this quilt—with or without the appliqué accents—is perfect for that special young lady in your life.

Finished Quilt Size: 63" x 63"   **Finished Block Size: 12" x 12"**

Materials

All yardages are based on 42"-wide fabric, unless otherwis noted. Each charm square needs measure at least 3⅞" x 3⅞".

32 charm squares *total* of assorted medium and/or dark purple fabrics for blocks

56 charm squares *total* of assorted medium and/or dark pink fabrics for block

200 charm squares *total* of assorted pale pink and/or lavender fabrics for blocks

⅔ yard of pale pink print for inner borders

1¼ yards of dark pink print fo outer border and binding

¼ yard of light green print for stem and leaf appliqués

⅛ yard *each* of dark purple and/or dark pink prints fo flower appliqués

Scraps of dark green print for leaf appliqués

4¼ yards of fabric for backing (2 widths pieced horizontally)

69" x 69" piece of batting

Cutting

All measurements include a ¼"-wide seam allowance. Cut all strips across the width of fabric (selvage to selvage).

From the assorted medium and/or dark purple charm squares, cut:

32 squares, 3⅞" x 3⅞"; cut once diagonally to yield 64 triangles

From the assorted medium and/or dark pink charm squares, cut:

56 squares, 3⅞" x 3⅞"; cut once diagonally to yield 112 triangles

From the assorted pale pink and/or lavender charm squares, cut:

112 squares, 3⅞" x 3⅞"; cut once diagonally to yield 224 triangles

88 squares, 3½" x 3½"

From the pale pink print, cut:

6 strips, 3½" x 42"

From the dark pink print, cut:

7 strips, 3½" x 42"

7 strips, 2" x 42"

Making the Blocks

1. Use the assorted medium and/or dark purple, assorted medium and/or dark pink, and the pale pink and/or lavender triangles; join triangle pairs along the long edges to make half-square-triangle units. Press the seam allowance toward the darker triangle. Make the number of units indicated for each color combination. Each unit should measure 3½" square. (You'll have 48 triangles left over to use in steps 4 and 5.)

Make 28. Make 16. Make 44.

Make 56. Make 32.

2. Arrange eight 3½" squares and eight half-square-triangle units from step 1 as shown. Be careful to position all the triangles correctly. Sew the squares and units into rows; press the seam allowances in alternate directions from row to row. Sew the rows together; press. Make four blocks.

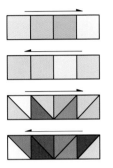 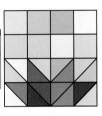

Make 4.

3. Arrange 16 half-square-triangle units from step 1 as shown. Be careful to position all the triangles correctly. Sew the units into rows; press the seam allowances in alternate directions from row to row. Sew the rows together; press. Make four purple Starflower blocks. Repeat to make five pink Starflower blocks.

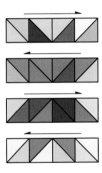

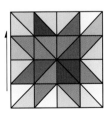 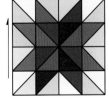

Make 5. Make 4.

4. Arrange and sew four triangles and six 3½" squares together in rows as shown; press. Sew the rows together; press. Make eight side-triangle units.

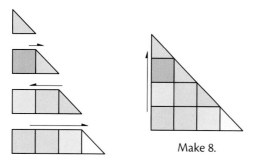

Make 8.

5. Arrange and sew four triangles and two 3½" squares together in rows as shown; press. Sew the rows together; press. Make four corner-triangle units.

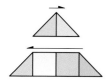 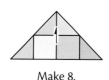

Make 8.

Quilt-Top Assembly

1. Refer to the assembly diagram to arrange the blocks and side-triangle units into diagonal rows as shown.

2. Sew the pieces in each row together; press. Sew the rows together; press the seams in one direction. Add the corner-triangle units to each corner.

3. Sew the 3½"-wide pale pink inner-border strips end to end to make one long strip. Measure the length of the quilt top through the center and cut two border strips to this size. Sew a strip to each side of the quilt top. Press toward the border. Measure the width of the quilt top through the center and cut two border strips to this size. Sew to the top and bottom of the quilt top. Press toward the border.

4. Repeat step 3 using the 3½"-wide dark pink strips to add the outer border to the sides, top, and bottom of the quilt top. Press the seams toward the outer border.

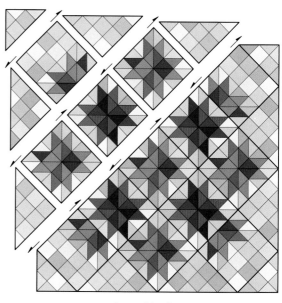

Assembly diagram

Adding the Appliqués

1. Make freezer-paper appliqués for the tulip center, outer petal, leaf, and stems, using the patterns and following the instructions on page 13. Refer to "Appliqué" on page 6 as needed.

2. Referring to the photo on page 10 and the appliqué placement guide, stitch all of the pieces to the quilt top.

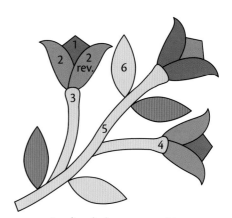

Appliqué placement guide.
Make 2 and 2 reversed.

Finishing the Quilt

1. Layer the quilt top with the batting and backing; baste the layers together.

2. Quilt as desired. I used the design on my backing fabric as a quilting design and quilted the majority of the quilt from the back. The loose swirls and loops were easy to quilt and gave the quilt a heavily quilted look, which I liked very much. Use the 2"-wide dark pink strips for the binding. Refer to "Binding Your Quilt" on page 8 as needed.

5
Stem
Make 2 and
2 reversed
from light
green.

Patterns do not
include seam
allowances.

4
Stem
Make 2 and 2 reversed
from light green.

3
Stem
Make 2 and 2 reversed
from light green.

1
Tulip center
Make 8 from
dark purple.
Make 4 from
dark pink.

2
Outer petal
Make 8 and 8 reversed
from dark pink.
Make 4 and 4 reversed
from dark purple.

6
Leaf
Make 8 from dark green.
Make 8 from light green.

SIMPLY CHARMING

 Don't be shy about mixing your boldest, brightest charm squares because anything goes in this quilt! With its decidedly scrappy appearance and prairie-point edging, it is indeed "simply charming!"

Materials

All yardages are based on 42"-wide fabric, unless otherwise noted. Each charm square needs to measure at least 3⅞" x 3⅞".

456 charm squares *total* of assorted white and/or beige prints for blocks
424 charm squares *total* of assorted medium and/or dark prints for blocks
7½ yards of fabric for backing (3 widths pieced horizontally)
84" x 84" square of batting

Finished Quilt Size: 78" x 78" (not including prairie points)

Finished Block Size: 9" x 9"   **Finished Border Block Sizes:** 12" x 12" and 9" x 12"

Cutting

All measurements include a ¼"-wide seam allowance.

From the assorted white and/or beige charm squares, cut:
100 squares, 3⅞" x 3⅞"; cut once diagonally
    to yield 200 triangles
356 squares, 3½" x 3½"

From the assorted medium and/or dark charm squares, cut:
100 squares, 3⅞" x 3⅞"; cut once diagonally
    to yield 200 triangles
324 squares, 3½" x 3½"

Making the Blocks

1. Use the white and/or beige and medium and/or dark triangles; join triangle pairs along the long edges to make 200 half-square-triangle units as shown. Press the seam allowance toward the darker triangle. Each unit should measure 3½" square.

Make 200.

2. Arrange half-square-triangle units and 3½" squares in rows as shown. Sew the squares and units into rows; press the seam allowances in alternate directions from row to row. Sew the rows together to complete the block; press. Make the number of blocks indicated for each combination of pieces.

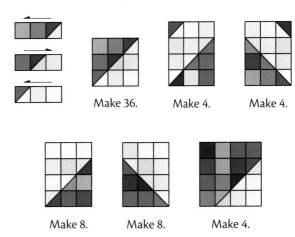

Make 36.   Make 4.   Make 4.

Make 8.   Make 8.   Make 4.

Quilt-Top Assembly

1. Refer to the assembly diagram to arrange the blocks into eight horizontal rows of eight blocks each.

2. Sew the blocks in each row together; press the seams in alternate directions from row to row. Sew the rows together; press the seams in one direction.

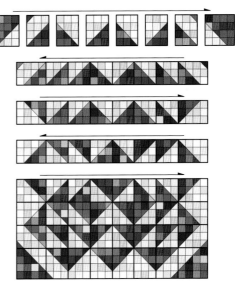

Assembly diagram

Finishing the Quilt

1. Layer the quilt top with the batting and backing; baste the layers together.

2. Quilt as desired; make sure no quilting stitches lie within ½" of the quilt edges to allow for the placement of the prairie points.

Adding the Prairie Points

1. To make prairie points, fold each remaining 3½" white and/or beige square and medium and/or dark square in half horizontally, wrong sides together; press. Then fold the two ends in toward the center on the diagonal as shown; press. Make 100 white and/or beige prairie points and 104 medium and/or dark prairie points.

Fold.   Fold.

2. Starting at one end of a quilt side, pin the cut edge of each medium and/or dark prairie point to the cut edge of the quilt top, aligning each prairie point with a square as shown and placing the folded side against the right side of the quilt top. Pin the backing out of the way. Sewing through the quilt top and batting only, stitch the prairie points to all four edges of the quilt, using a ¼"-wide seam allowance.

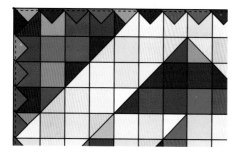

3. Center each of the white and/or beige prairie points between two of the medium and/or dark prairie points as shown. Align the cut edges and pin in place. Sew the prairie points to all four edges of the quilt, using a scant ¼"-wide seam allowance.

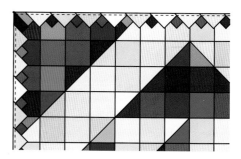

4. Trim the batting close to the stitching. Fold the prairie points out, turning the seam allowance in toward the batting, and lightly press on the right side. Trim the backing fabric so that it extends ⅜" beyond the edge of the quilt top. Then turn the seam allowance of the backing under, covering the seam allowance and the lines of stitches. Finish the back of the quilt using a blind stitch. Add quilting stitches along the edge of the quilt if necessary.

INTERLOCKING SQUARES

Is there a special man in your life who deserves a quilt of his own? This quilt has a distinctly masculine feel, but if blue gives you the "blues," experiment with charm squares in shades of your favorite color.

Finished Quilt Size: 80½" x 89"

Materials

All yardages are based on 42"-wide fabric, unless otherwise noted. Each charm square needs to measure at least 3½" x 3½".

190 charm squares *total* of assorted light blue prints for blocks

206 charm squares *total* of assorted dark blue prints for blocks

5⅛ yards white-and-blue print for blocks, side triangles, and corner triangles

8 yards of fabric for backing (3 widths pieced horizontally)

⅝ yard of dark blue fabric for binding

87" x 95" rectangle of batting

Cutting

All measurements include a ¼"-wide seam allowance. Cut all strips across the width of fabric (selvage to selvage).

From the dark blue charm squares, cut:
206 squares, 3½" x 3½"

From the light blue charm squares, cut:
190 squares, 3½" x 3½"

From the white-and-blue print, cut:
43 strips, 3½" x 42"; crosscut into 463 squares, 3½" x 3½"
19 squares, 5½" x 5½"; cut twice diagonally to yield 76 triangles
2 squares, 3" x 3"; cut once diagonally to yield 4 triangles

From the dark blue for binding, cut:
9 strips, 2" x 42"

Making Quarter-Circle Units

1. Refer to "Quarter-Circle Units" on page 7 as needed. Make freezer-paper templates of the quarter-circle shape by tracing the pattern at right. Cut out the quantity indicated on the pattern.

2. Prepare and cut out 52 assorted dark blue shapes and 48 assorted light blue shapes, adding a ¼"-wide seam allowance to the curved edge only. Fold the seam allowance under and baste. Pin each quarter-circle shape to a 3½" white-and-blue square, aligning the straight edges. Hand stitch along the curved edge with matching thread.

Make 52.

Make 48.

Quilt-Top Assembly

1. Refer to the assembly diagram to arrange the quarter-circle blocks, dark blue squares, light blue squares, white-and-blue squares, and the 5½" triangles into diagonal rows as shown.

2. Sew the pieces in each row together; press the seams in alternate directions from row to row. Sew the

rows together; press the seams in one direction. Add the 3" triangles to each corner.

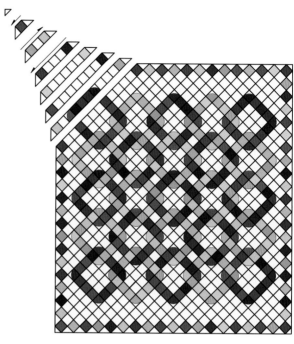
Assembly diagram

Finishing the Quilt

1. Layer the quilt top with the batting and backing; baste the layers together.

2. Quilt as desired. Use the 2"-wide dark blue strips for the binding. Refer to "Binding Your Quilt" on page 8 as needed.

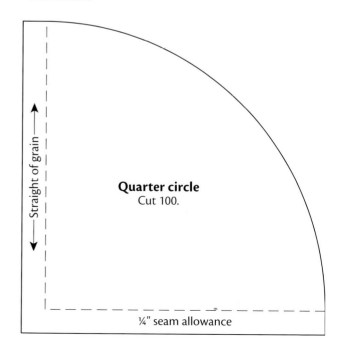

Straight of grain →

Quarter circle
Cut 100.

¼" seam allowance

When assembling a quilt top, sewing smaller individual pieces into rows, instead of larger pieced blocks, can be tricky. It's extremely easy to miscount and lose track of where you are, especially when dealing with hundreds of squares. To help keep track of the pieces and completed rows, copy the diagram below and use a highlighter to mark off each piece as you stitch.

HEARTS AND FLOWERS

Nothing says "Love" like hearts and flowers. The pieced multiprint background accentuates the appliqué perfectly.

Finished Quilt Size: 71" x 81½"   Finished Block Size: 10½" x 10½"

Finished Border Block Sizes: 10½" x 9¼" and 9¼" x 9¼"

Materials

All yardages are based on 42"-wide fabric, unless otherwise noted. Each charm square needs to measure at least 4" x 4".

324 charm squares *total* of assorted medium and/or dark prints for blocks and heart, butterfly, and flower appliqués

336 charm squares *total* of assorted off-white and/or beige prints for blocks

½ yard of dark green print for stem, vine, flower, and leaf appliqués

Scraps of light green prints for flower and leaf appliqués

Scraps of assorted yellow prints for flower appliqués

¾ yard of blue fabric for bias binding

5½ yards of fabric for backing (2 widths pieced vertically)

77" x 88" piece of batting

⅜"-wide bias bar

Cutting

All measurements include a ¼"-wide seam allowance. Template patterns for pieces A, B, and C are on page 24. For detailed instructions, refer to "Templates" on page 6.

From the assorted medium and/or dark charm squares, cut:
126 squares, 4" x 4"
30 pieces with template A
26 pieces with template B
26 pieces with template B reversed
4 pieces with template C

From the assorted off-white and/or beige charm squares, cut:
336 squares, 4" x 4"

From the dark green fabric, cut:
235" of 1¼"-wide bias strips

From the blue fabric, cut:
375" of 2"-wide bias strips

Making Quarter-Circle Units

1. Refer to "Quarter-Circle Units" on page 7 as needed. Make freezer-paper templates of the quarter-circle shape by tracing the pattern on page 23. Cut out the quantity indicated on the pattern.

2. Prepare and cut out 44 assorted off-white or beige shapes, adding a ¼"-wide seam allowance to the curved edge only. Fold the seam allowance under and baste. Pin each quarter-circle shape to a 4" assorted medium or dark square, aligning the straight edges. Hand stitch along the curved edge with matching thread.

Making the Blocks

1. Sew nine 4" off-white and/or beige squares together in rows; press. Sew the rows together as shown to make 30 Nine Patch blocks; press.

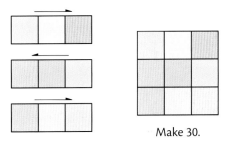

Make 30.

2. Sew three 4" medium and/or dark print squares, one 4" off-white and/or beige square, two quarter-circle units, one assorted print B piece and one B reversed piece, and one assorted print A piece together in rows; press. Sew the rows together; press. Make 22 side border blocks.

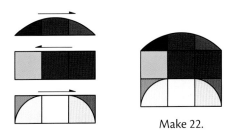

Make 22.

3. Sew four 4" medium and/or dark print squares, one assorted print B piece and one B reversed piece, two assorted print A pieces, and one assorted print C piece together in rows; press. Sew the rows together; press. Make 4 corner blocks.

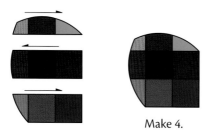

Make 4.

Adding the Appliqués

You'll be using the remaining 4" medium and/or dark print squares, so don't discard the scraps. They can be used for the smaller appliqué shapes.

1. Make freezer-paper appliqués for the heart, flower petal, flower center, leaf, bud center, outer bud, and butterfly using the patterns and following the instructions on pages 23–24. Refer to "Appliqué" on page 6 as needed.

2. Arrange six heart shapes in the center of a Nine Patch block as shown. Stitch in place using matching thread. Make 14 blocks. (The remaining Nine Patch blocks will be used in step 1 of "Quilt-Top Assembly.")

Make 14.

Quilt-Top Assembly

1. Refer to the assembly diagram to arrange the appliquéd Nine Patch blocks, remaining Nine Patch blocks, side border blocks, and corner blocks into eight horizontal rows of seven blocks each.

2. Sew the blocks in each row together; press the seams in alternate directions from row to row. Sew the rows together; press the seams in one direction.

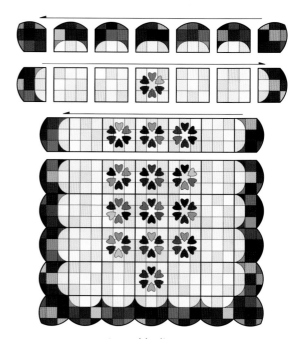

Assembly diagram

3. Referring to the photo on page 20 for placement, arrange six of the heart shapes from step 1 of "Adding the Appliqués" on the left side of the quilt, centering them as shown. Stitch in place using matching thread. Repeat to stitch six heart shapes to the right side.

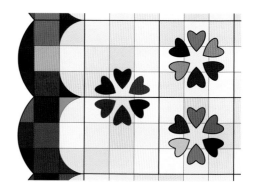

4. Stitch the 1¼" dark green bias strips together to make one long strip. Refer to "Bias Stems and Vines" on page 7 and use the ⅜"-wide bias bar to make a bias tube. From the long tube, cut 16 stems, each 8" in length. For the vine, cut the remaining tube into four 26" lengths. Refer to the photo and the placement guide below to arrange and then stitch the stems and vines in place using matching thread.

Stem and vine placement guide

5. Referring to the photo for placement, arrange the appliqué shapes for the flower petals, flower centers, leaves, bud centers, outer buds, and butterfly, prepared in step 1 of "Adding the Appliqué," on the quilt top. Stitch in place using matching thread.

6. After all the appliqué work is complete, gently press the quilt top.

Finishing the Quilt

1. Layer the quilt top with the batting and backing; baste the layers together.

2. Quilt as desired. The quilt shown was hand quilted with an outline stitch around the appliqués and on each side of the straight seam lines. A heart motif was quilted between the appliqué hearts.

3. Use the 2"-wide blue bias strips for the binding. Refer to "Binding Your Quilt" on page 8 as needed.

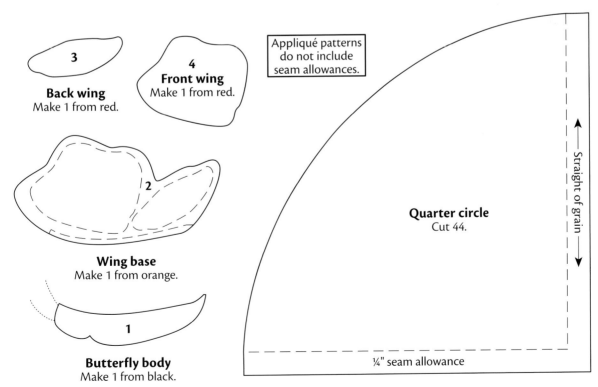

3
Back wing
Make 1 from red.

4
Front wing
Make 1 from red.

Appliqué patterns do not include seam allowances.

2
Wing base
Make 1 from orange.

1
Butterfly body
Make 1 from black.

Quarter circle
Cut 44.

Straight of grain

¼" seam allowance

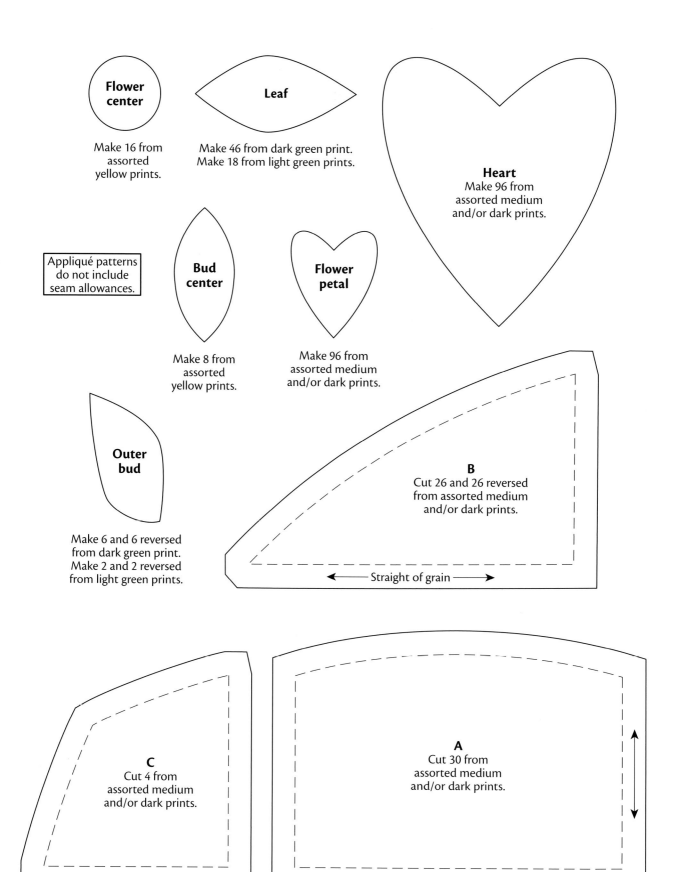

Flower center

Make 16 from assorted yellow prints.

Leaf

Make 46 from dark green print.
Make 18 from light green prints.

Heart
Make 96 from assorted medium and/or dark prints.

Appliqué patterns do not include seam allowances.

Bud center

Make 8 from assorted yellow prints.

Flower petal

Make 96 from assorted medium and/or dark prints.

Outer bud

Make 6 and 6 reversed from dark green print.
Make 2 and 2 reversed from light green prints.

B
Cut 26 and 26 reversed from assorted medium and/or dark prints.

← Straight of grain →

C
Cut 4 from assorted medium and/or dark prints.

A
Cut 30 from assorted medium and/or dark prints.

¼" seam allowance

COLOR IN LAYERS

 Layers and layers of color! What more could a quilter want?

Finished Quilt Size: 61" x 61"   **Finished Block Size:** 9" x 9"

Materials

All yardages are based on 42"-wide fabric, unless otherwise noted. Each charm square needs to measure at least 3½" x 3½".

24 charm squares in *each* of the following 13 color families: dark pink, dark purple, bright orange, pastel yellow, pastel blue, dark blue, dark rust, dark green, pastel lavender, pastel pink, burgundy, teal, and dark brown, for blocks. You'll have a total of 312 squares.*

120 charm squares of assorted black prints for blocks

¾ yard *total* of assorted black prints for border

½ yard of purple fabric for bias binding

4 yards of fabric for backing (2 widths pieced horizontally)

67" x 67" piece of batting

Choose a range of value within each color family.

Cutting

All measurements include a ¼"-wide seam allowance. The template pattern for piece A is on page 28. For detailed instructions, refer to "Templates" on page 6.

From *each* color family of 24 charm squares, cut:
24 squares, 3½" x 3½" (312 total)

From the assorted black charm squares, cut:
120 squares, 3½" x 3½"

From the assorted black prints, cut:
12 pieces with template A

From the purple fabric, cut:
255" of 2"-wide bias strips

Making the Blocks

1. Refer to "Quarter-Circle Units" on page 7 as needed. Make freezer-paper templates of the quarter-circle shape by tracing the pattern on page 28. Cut out the quantity indicated on the pattern.

2. Refer to the illustrations below and the photo on page 25 for color combinations. Cut out each shape, adding a ¼"-wide seam allowance to the curved edge only. Fold the seam allowance under and baste. Pin each quarter-circle shape to a 3½" square, aligning the straight edges. Hand stitch along the curved edge with matching thread. Make the number indicated for each color combination.

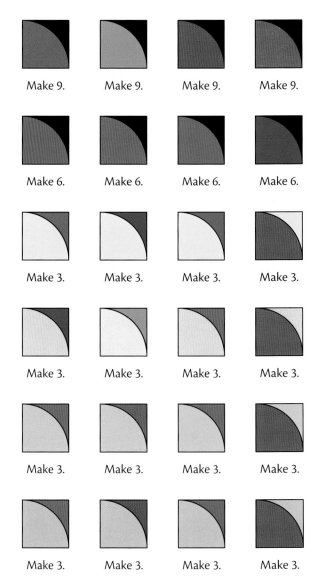

Make 9. Make 9. Make 9. Make 9.

Make 6. Make 6. Make 6. Make 6.

Make 3. Make 3. Make 3. Make 3.

Make 3. Make 3. Make 3. Make 3.

Make 3. Make 3. Make 3. Make 3.

Make 3. Make 3. Make 3. Make 3.

3. Arrange three quarter-circle units and six 3½" squares in the color combinations as shown. Stitch the pieces in each row together; press. Then stitch the rows together to complete the block. Repeat with the remaining units to make the number of blocks indicated for each color combination.

Quilt-Top Assembly

1. Refer to the assembly diagram to arrange the blocks into six horizontal rows of six blocks each.

2. Sew the blocks in each row together; press the seams in alternate directions from row to row. Sew the rows together; press the seams in one direction.

3. Sew three black A pieces together along the short ends to make one border strip. Make four. Align the straight edge of each border strip with the raw edges of the quilt, right sides together. Stitch in place using a ¼"-wide seam allowance. Sew opposite sides first, and then the remaining two edges. Press the seam allowances toward the border.

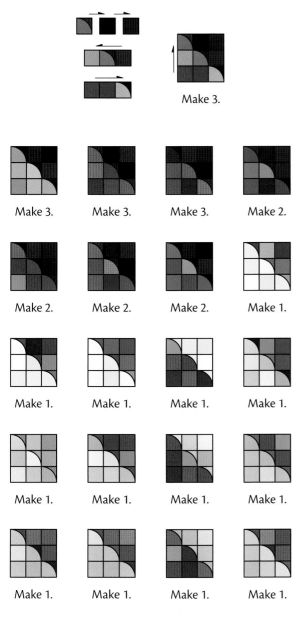

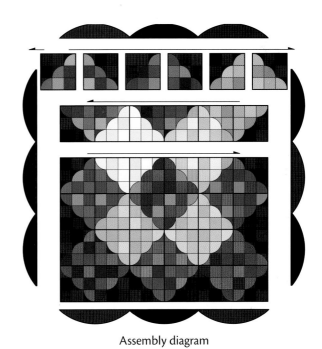

Assembly diagram

Finishing the Quilt

1. Layer the quilt top with the batting and backing; baste the layers together.

2. Quilt as desired. Use the 2"-wide purple bias strips for the binding. Refer to "Binding Your Quilt" on page 8 as needed.

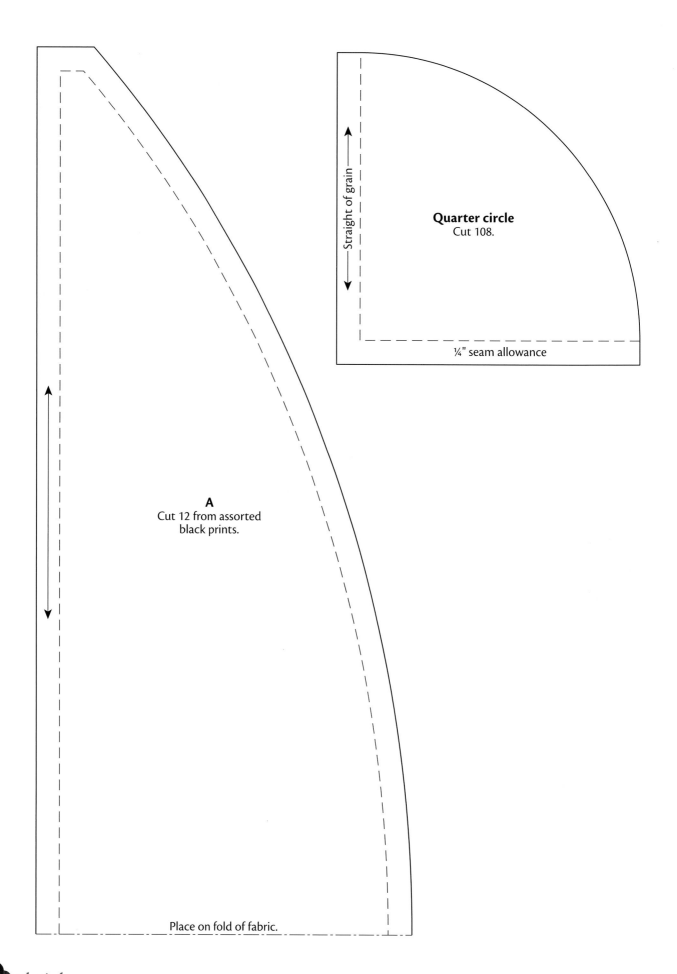

Straight of grain

Quarter circle
Cut 108.

¼" seam allowance

A
Cut 12 from assorted
black prints.

Place on fold of fabric.

PRETTY IN PINK

What could be prettier than pink, besides lots of it? If you don't "think pink," this ultrafeminine quilt would be just as lovely in your favorite color.

Finished Quilt Size: 69" x 69"   **Finished Block Size:** 9" x 9"

Finished Border Block Sizes: 12" x 12" and 9" x 12"

Materials

All yardages are based on 42"-wide fabric, unless otherwise noted. Each charm square needs to measure at least 3½" x 3½".

332 charm squares of assorted pink prints for blocks

3⅛ yards of small-scale white print for blocks

1 yard of medium green print for vine, stem, bud, and leaf appliqués

Scraps of dark green fabric for leaf and bud appliqués

Scraps of assorted pink prints for heart, flower, and bud appliqués

Scraps of assorted yellow prints for flower center appliqués

¾ yard of pink fabric for binding

4½ yards of fabric for backing (2 widths pieced horizontally)

75" x 75" piece of batting

¼"-wide bias bar

Cutting

All measurements include a ¼"-wide seam allowance. The template pattern for piece C is on page 32. For detailed instructions, refer to "Templates" on page 6.

From the assorted pink charm squares, cut:
292 squares, 3½" x 3½"
40 pieces with template C

From the white print, cut:
27 strips, 3½" x 42"; crosscut into 297 squares,
    3½" x 3½"
16 pieces with template C

From the medium green print, cut:
670" of 1"-wide bias strips

From the pink fabric for binding, cut:
370" of 2"-wide bias strips

Making the Blocks

1. Refer to "Quarter-Circle Units" on page 7 as needed. Make freezer-paper templates of the A and B shapes by tracing the patterns on page 22. Cut out the quantity indicated on the patterns.

2. Using the 3½" pink squares and the templates from step 1, prepare and cut out 68 A shapes and 8 B shapes, adding a ¼"-wide seam allowance to the curved edge only. Fold the seam allowance under and baste. Pin each shape to a 3½" white square, aligning the straight edges as shown. Hand stitch along the curved edge with matching thread. Repeat using the remaining 3½" white squares to make 36 A shapes and 8 B shapes. Pin and stitch each white shape to a 3½" pink square.

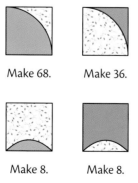

Make 68.   Make 36.

Make 8.   Make 8.

3. Refer to the illustrations below and the photo on page 29 for placement. Arrange the A and B units from step 2, pink and/or white 3½" squares, and the pink and/or white C pieces as shown. Stitch the pieces in each row together; press the seams in alternate directions from row to row. Then stitch the rows together to complete the block. Make the number of blocks indicated for each combination of pieces.

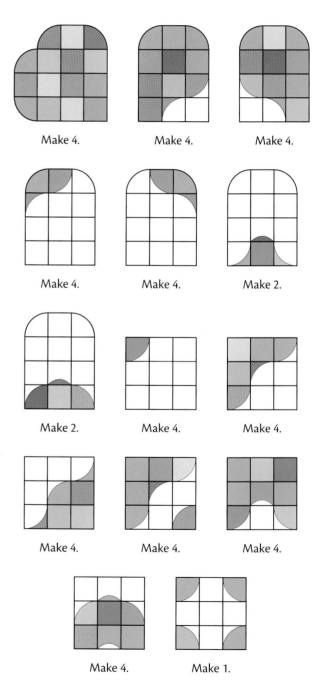

Make 4.   Make 4.   Make 4.

Make 4.   Make 4.   Make 2.

Make 2.   Make 4.   Make 4.

Make 4.   Make 4.   Make 4.

Make 4.   Make 1.

Quilt-Top Assembly

1. Refer to the assembly diagram to arrange the blocks into seven horizontal rows of seven blocks each.

2. Sew the blocks in each row together; press the seams in alternate directions from row to row. Sew the rows together; press the seams in one direction.

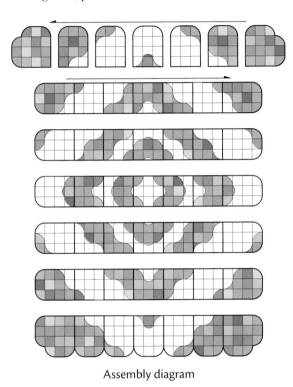

Assembly diagram

Adding the Appliqués

1. Make freezer-paper appliqués for the heart, flower, flower center, leaf, inner bud, and outer bud, using the patterns and following the instructions on page 32. Refer to "Appliqué" on page 6 as needed.

2. Stitch the 1" medium green bias strips together to make one long strip. Refer to "Bias Stems and Vines" on page 7 and use the ¼"-wide bias bar to make a bias tube. From the long tube, cut 48 stems, each 6" in length. For the vines, cut the remaining tube into four 54" lengths and four 28" lengths. Referring to the photo, stitch the stems and vines in place using matching thread.

3. Referring to the photo for placement, arrange the heart, flower, flower center, leaf, inner bud, and outer bud appliqués, prepared in step 1, on the quilt top. Stitch them in place using matching thread.

4. After all the appliqué work is complete, gently press the quilt top.

Finishing the Quilt

1. Layer the quilt top with the batting and backing; baste the layers together.

2. Quilt as desired. This quilt was hand quilted. The pink squares were quilted using the pattern shown below, and outline quilting was added around the appliqué hearts, flowers, leaves and stems.

3. Use the 2"-wide pink bias strips for the binding. Refer to "Binding Your Quilt" on page 8 as needed.

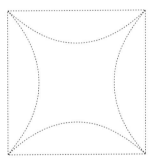

Quilting motif for pink squares

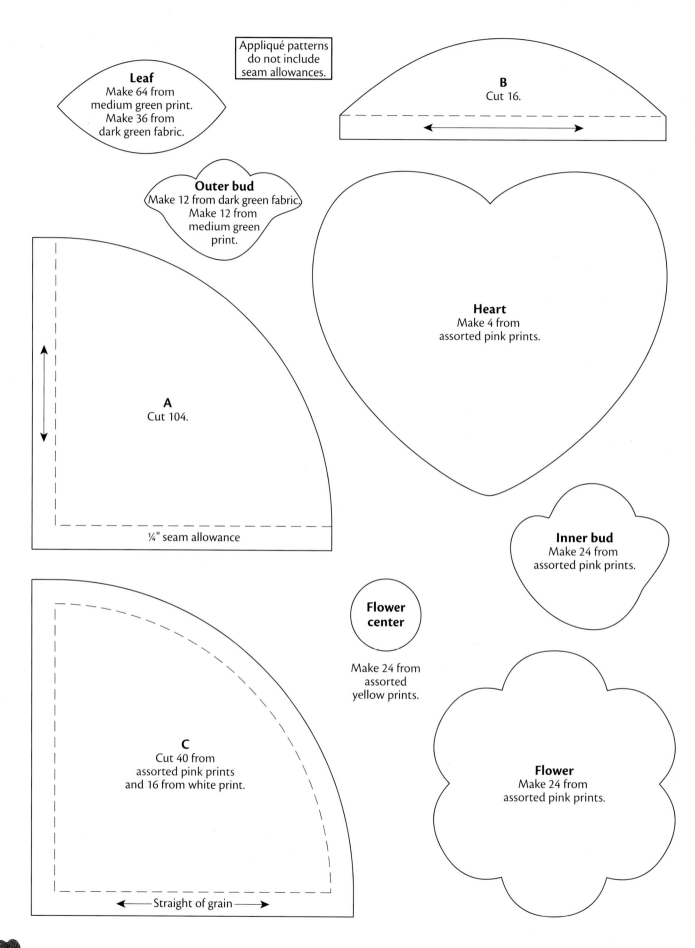

Leaf
Make 64 from
medium green print.
Make 36 from
dark green fabric.

Appliqué patterns
do not include
seam allowances.

B
Cut 16.

Outer bud
Make 12 from dark green fabric.
Make 12 from
medium green
print.

Heart
Make 4 from
assorted pink prints.

A
Cut 104.

¼" seam allowance

Inner bud
Make 24 from
assorted pink prints.

Flower
center

Make 24 from
assorted
yellow prints.

C
Cut 40 from
assorted pink prints
and 16 from white print.

Flower
Make 24 from
assorted pink prints.

Straight of grain